Madelynn

My Hospital
JOURNEY
It's Okay To Be Afraid

Cover and interior design by Eileen Cueno
Illustrations by Van Kevin Opura

Published in the United States of America

ISBN: 9781799027683
1. Juvenile Nonfiction / Health & Daily Living / Diseases, Illnesses & Injuries
2. Juvenile Nonfiction / Social Issues / Emotions & Feelings
16.06.20

THIS BOOK BELONGS TO:

_____

1
My Life Begins

I was born on October 28, 2003. I have a twin sister. My mother was in the hospital for a long time before we were born. We were born too early. We stayed in the hospital for three months before we were allowed to go home. Our middle names are Faith and Hope.

My mom and dad told us all about how our lives started. When we came home, we were very small and took a lot of medicines and slept all day. Mom and Dad took very good care of us. My big brother Jake was very jealous.

Because we were so small and born too soon, we had some problems. We both had trouble with our hearts, and I was missing some ribs. It was hard for me to breathe and walk. I had to use oxygen for the first few years. My sister Maddison was doing well, but I still had some problems. We both kept growing, and when I turned three years old, everything changed.

2

My First Surgery

When I was three years old, some very nice doctors wanted to help me. San Antonio was a very special place. At the children's hospital, they could help kids who have missing ribs. People from all over the world go there to get help. It was the only place for kids to go for this kind of surgery.

When I was getting ready for my first titanium rib surgery, the doctors said I needed to fix a different problem first. My neck and spinal cord had a problem. I needed a special surgery that would fix that problem.

After the surgery, I couldn't move my head at all. I had special metal rods that held my head still so I could not hurt my spinal cord. The surgery was very hard but a big success. Now I was ready for my new ribs!

3
I Hate Preop Day!

When we went back to the hospital for my first titanium rib surgery, I was nervous and frightened. The day before surgery is called preop day. At preop day, they would take many x-rays, CAT scans, and MRIs. My dad joked that we would both glow in the dark. He was always with me during my tests. They would also take my blood out of my arm with a needle. This is the part I hate the most. It hurts every time. My daddy holds me very tight when they do this.

After preop is over, we leave the hospital and always go to lunch and see a special movie.

Madelynn Faith Niles

My Hospital JOURNEY

It's Okay To Be Afraid

Cover and interior design by Eileen Cueno
Illustrations by Van Kevin Opura

Published in the United States of America

ISBN: 9781799027683
1. Juvenile Nonfiction / Health & Daily Living / Diseases, Illnesses & Injuries
2. Juvenile Nonfiction / Social Issues / Emotions & Feelings
16.06.20

THIS BOOK BELONGS TO:

_____

1
My Life Begins

I was born on October 28, 2003. I have a twin sister. My mother was in the hospital for a long time before we were born. We were born too early. We stayed in the hospital for three months before we were allowed to go home. Our middle names are Faith and Hope.

My mom and dad told us all about how our lives started. When we came home, we were very small and took a lot of medicines and slept all day. Mom and Dad took very good care of us. My big brother Jake was very jealous.

Because we were so small and born too soon, we had some problems. We both had trouble with our hearts, and I was missing some ribs. It was hard for me to breathe and walk. I had to use oxygen for the first few years. My sister Maddison was doing well, but I still had some problems. We both kept growing, and when I turned three years old, everything changed.

2

My First Surgery

When I was three years old, some very nice doctors wanted to help me. San Antonio was a very special place. At the children's hospital, they could help kids who have missing ribs. People from all over the world go there to get help. It was the only place for kids to go for this kind of surgery.

When I was getting ready for my first titanium rib surgery, the doctors said I needed to fix a different problem first. My neck and spinal cord had a problem. I needed a special surgery that would fix that problem.

After the surgery, I couldn't move my head at all. I had special metal rods that held my head still so I could not hurt my spinal cord. The surgery was very hard but a big success. Now I was ready for my new ribs!

3
I Hate Preop Day!

When we went back to the hospital for my first titanium rib surgery, I was nervous and frightened. The day before surgery is called preop day. At preop day, they would take many x-rays, CAT scans, and MRIs. My dad joked that we would both glow in the dark. He was always with me during my tests. They would also take my blood out of my arm with a needle. This is the part I hate the most. It hurts every time. My daddy holds me very tight when they do this.

After preop is over, we leave the hospital and always go to lunch and see a special movie.

The next day is the big day—surgery day. I don't remember all my surgeries because I have had them every six months since I was three years old. But on surgery day, we go to the hospital very early. I put on special pajamas, and I get scared. My mom and dad stay with me as long as they can. We do a few more tests, and then I sit on my dad's lap as he rides in a wheelchair to surgery.

We go to a special room where I lay in a bed and get a visit from all the doctors. They try to make me laugh, but I still get scared. They give me special medicine that makes me sleepy and silly. When it is time for surgery, they push the bed to the operating room. My mom and dad walk with me as far as they are allowed. One of the doctors sings songs to me on the way to the operating room. My mom and dad kiss me good-bye and promise to be there when I wake up.

In the surgery room, it smells funny and is cold. There are many people surrounding me. They lay me down on a special bed that I don't like. It is very hard. A nice doctor talks to me and puts a mask over my face to make me sleep. The mask smells like monkey butt.

Just as soon as I fall asleep, I start waking up in another room. My mom and dad are there with me. I am very sleepy, and I am in pain. The nurse asks me if I need medicine for the pain. Sometimes I say yes. After a while, I get to go to my own hospital room.

4

Let's Do a Marathon

Mom and Dad walk alongside my bed on the way to
my room. On the sixth floor, all the kids' rooms have
different-colored doors. We always take a guess what
the color of my room will be. My bed is pushed into the
room, and my dad scoops me gently over to the new
bed. I sleep for a few hours. I wake up in pain, and the
nurse gives me medicine through my IV. By the end of the
day, I am ready to walk. The doctors are happy because
I always get out of bed way before the other kids. The
rooms are all full of titanium rib kids.

We begin to walk the halls very slowly. We walk all around the unit. I have favorite places to go. Every time we pass the coyote from the San Antonio Spurs, we smack him. Sometimes the San Antonio Spurs visit the kids in the unit, and once, they gave me a basketball. Another place we visit is the playroom. I like to color and play games. My most favorite place is our secret clubhouse. It is a small place that goes to the stairs. Our voices echo, and there are pictures on the walls of the stairs. We have been going there for many years. We only show a few people our secret clubhouse.

When I first started having surgery, I would stay in the hospital for about a week. But now that I am older and stronger, I usually only stay for one or two days. The doctors visit me every morning to see how I am doing. I like to show them I can jump and stand on one leg. It usually scares them. They call me Supergirl.

5

Going Home

The morning that the doctor says we can go home is awesome. Someone takes us to x-ray in a wheelchair so that the doctor can see that everything from the surgery is okay. Once the doctor sees the x-rays, the nurse comes to take out my IV. I don't like when they do this because it hurts. When we leave the hospital, I like to go to the gift shop and get a present for my brother and sister. My favorite part of the whole trip is when my daddy brings the car to the front of the hospital and gently scoops me up and sits me in the car.

Now that I am eleven years old, the doctors say I might only need surgery every nine months. This makes me very happy. I would like to be a doctor that helps children when I grow up, just like they helped me.

THE END

Made in the USA
Coppell, TX
23 April 2021

The next day is the big day—surgery day. I don't remember all my surgeries because I have had them every six months since I was three years old. But on surgery day, we go to the hospital very early. I put on special pajamas, and I get scared. My mom and dad stay with me as long as they can. We do a few more tests, and then I sit on my dad's lap as he rides in a wheelchair to surgery.

We go to a special room where I lay in a bed and get a visit from all the doctors. They try to make me laugh, but I still get scared. They give me special medicine that makes me sleepy and silly. When it is time for surgery, they push the bed to the operating room. My mom and dad walk with me as far as they are allowed. One of the doctors sings songs to me on the way to the operating room. My mom and dad kiss me good-bye and promise to be there when I wake up.

In the surgery room, it smells funny and is cold. There are many people surrounding me. They lay me down on a special bed that I don't like. It is very hard. A nice doctor talks to me and puts a mask over my face to make me sleep. The mask smells like monkey butt.

Just as soon as I fall asleep, I start waking up in another room. My mom and dad are there with me. I am very sleepy, and I am in pain. The nurse asks me if I need medicine for the pain. Sometimes I say yes. After a while, I get to go to my own hospital room.

4

Let's Do a Marathon

Mom and Dad walk alongside my bed on the way to my room. On the sixth floor, all the kids' rooms have different-colored doors. We always take a guess what the color of my room will be. My bed is pushed into the room, and my dad scoops me gently over to the new bed. I sleep for a few hours. I wake up in pain, and the nurse gives me medicine through my IV. By the end of the day, I am ready to walk. The doctors are happy because I always get out of bed way before the other kids. The rooms are all full of titanium rib kids.

We begin to walk the halls very slowly. We walk all around the unit. I have favorite places to go. Every time we pass the coyote from the San Antonio Spurs, we smack him. Sometimes the San Antonio Spurs visit the kids in the unit, and once, they gave me a basketball. Another place we visit is the playroom. I like to color and play games. My most favorite place is our secret clubhouse. It is a small place that goes to the stairs. Our voices echo, and there are pictures on the walls of the stairs. We have been going there for many years. We only show a few people our secret clubhouse.

When I first started having surgery, I would stay in the hospital for about a week. But now that I am older and stronger, I usually only stay for one or two days. The doctors visit me every morning to see how I am doing. I like to show them I can jump and stand on one leg. It usually scares them. They call me Supergirl.

5
Going Home

The morning that the doctor says we can go home is awesome. Someone takes us to x-ray in a wheelchair so that the doctor can see that everything from the surgery is okay. Once the doctor sees the x-rays, the nurse comes to take out my IV. I don't like when they do this because it hurts. When we leave the hospital, I like to go to the gift shop and get a present for my brother and sister. My favorite part of the whole trip is when my daddy brings the car to the front of the hospital and gently scoops me up and sits me in the car.

Now that I am eleven years old, the doctors say I might only need surgery every nine months. This makes me very happy. I would like to be a doctor that helps children when I grow up, just like they helped me.

THE END

Made in the USA
Coppell, TX
23 April 2021